BLUE WHALES

by Mari Schuh

Raintree is an imprint of Capstone Global Library Limited, a company incorporated in England and Wales having its registered office at 264 Banbury Road, Oxford, OX2 7DY – Registered company number: 6695582

www.raintree.co.uk
myorders@raintree.co.uk

Text © Capstone Global Library Limited 2021
The moral rights of the proprietor have been asserted.

All rights reserved. No part of this publication may be reproduced in any form or by any means (including photocopying or storing it in any medium by electronic means and whether or not transiently or incidentally to some other use of this publication) without the written permission of the copyright owner, except in accordance with the provisions of the Copyright, Designs and Patents Act 1988 or under the terms of a licence issued by the Copyright Licensing Agency, Barnard's Inn, 86 Fetter Lane, London, EC4A 1EN (www.cla.co.uk). Applications for the copyright owner's written permission should be addressed to the publisher.

Edited by Mandy Robbins
Designed by Dina Her
Original illustrations © Capstone Global Library Limited 2021
Picture research by Morgan Walters
Production by Tori Abraham
Originated by Capstone Global Library Ltd

978 1 4747 9489 3 (hardback)
978 1 4747 9618 7 (paperback)

British Library Cataloguing in Publication Data
A full catalogue record for this book is available from the British Library.

Acknowledgements
We would like to thank the following for permission to reproduce photographs: Alamy: Francois Gohier / VWPics, 7, Nature Picture Library, 8, 17, WaterFrame, 21; Getty Images: Doug Perrine, 12, Mark Carwardine, 13; iStockphoto: amac00, 5; Minden Pictures: Flip Nicklin, spread 26-27, Luis Quinta, 14; Newscom: Album/Gus Regalado, spread 10-11, Flip Nicklin/Minden Pictures, 9, Francois Gohier/VWPics, 1, McPHOTO/picture alliance / blickwinkel/M, 25; Shutterstock: Andrea Izzotti, 16, Andrew Sutton, Cover, John Tunney, 19, Nicole Helgason, 28, Rich Carey, 22

Every effort has been made to contact copyright holders of material reproduced in this book. Any omissions will be rectified in subsequent printings if notice is given to the publisher.

All the internet addresses (URLs) given in this book were valid at the time of going to press. However, due to the dynamic nature of the internet, some addresses may have changed, or sites may have changed or ceased to exist since publication. While the author and publisher regret any inconvenience this may cause readers, no responsibility for any such changes can be accepted by either the author or the publisher.

Printed and bound in India.

Contents

Amazing blue whales 4

Where blue whales live 6

Blue whale bodies 10

Eating and drinking 16

What blue whales do 20

Dangers to blue whales 26

    Fast facts 29

    Glossary 30

    Find out more 31

    Index 32

Words in **bold** are in the glossary.

Amazing blue whales

A blue whale swims by. It blows air out of its **blowholes**. Whoosh! A stream of air and water shoots up. It goes 9 metres (30 feet) high!

The whale takes in air through the holes. Then it dives down.

Whales are **mammals**. Mammals are **warm-blooded**. Their body temperature does not change. Females feed milk to their young.

A blue whale blows air out of its blowholes.

Where blue whales live

About 10,000 to 25,000 blue whales live in the world. They live in every ocean. The biggest ones live in the cold Southern Ocean.

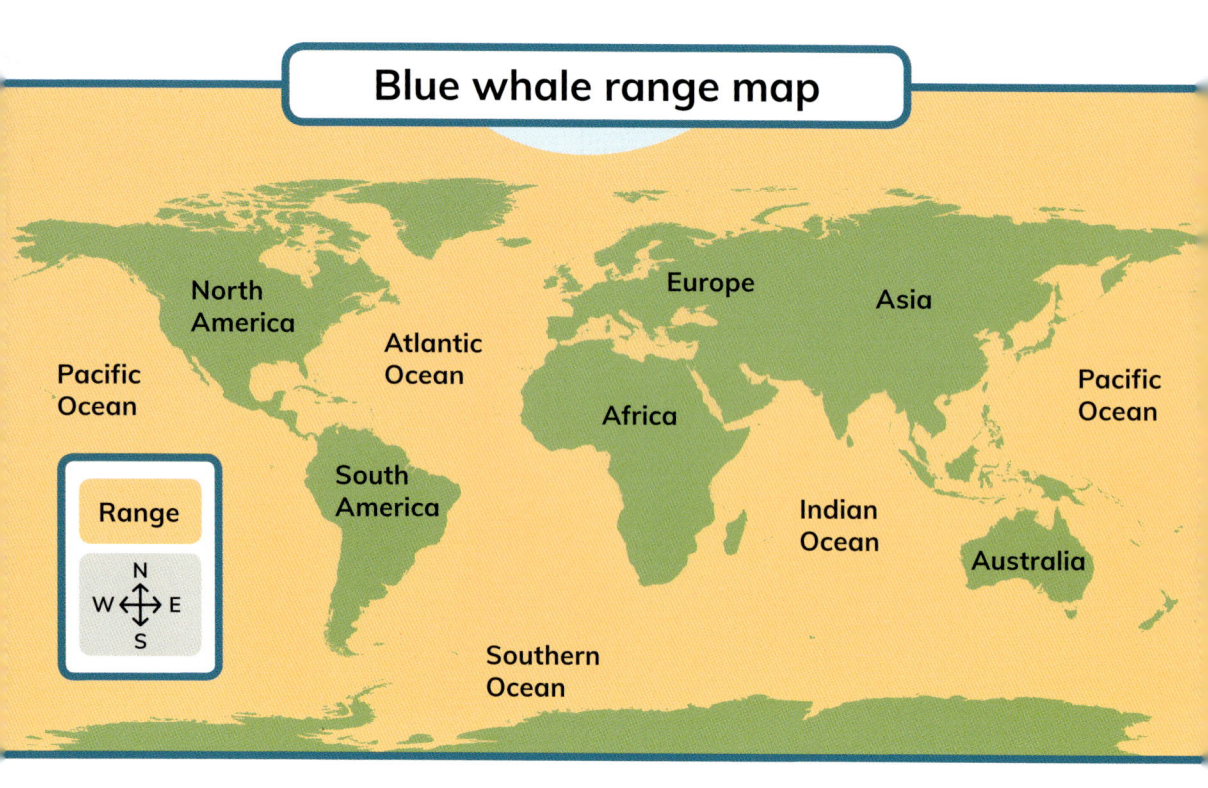

Blue whale range map

- North America
- Pacific Ocean
- Atlantic Ocean
- South America
- Europe
- Africa
- Asia
- Indian Ocean
- Pacific Ocean
- Australia
- Southern Ocean

Range

N, W, E, S

Most blue whales live in the southern half of the world. Some live in the northern half.

Blue whales often swim alone or in pairs. They also swim in small groups.

Blue whales eating

Blue whales often swim in cold water. They live there in the summer. They eat a lot of food at that time.

During the day, the whales dive to find food. At night, they eat near the surface of the water.

Many blue whales **migrate** in winter. They go to warmer waters. The whales **mate** there. Young whales are born. They grow up in the warm water.

Blue whale bodies

Blue whales are huge. They are the biggest animal that has ever lived. They are bigger than any dinosaurs were. They can be up to 30 metres (100 feet) long. That is longer than two buses!

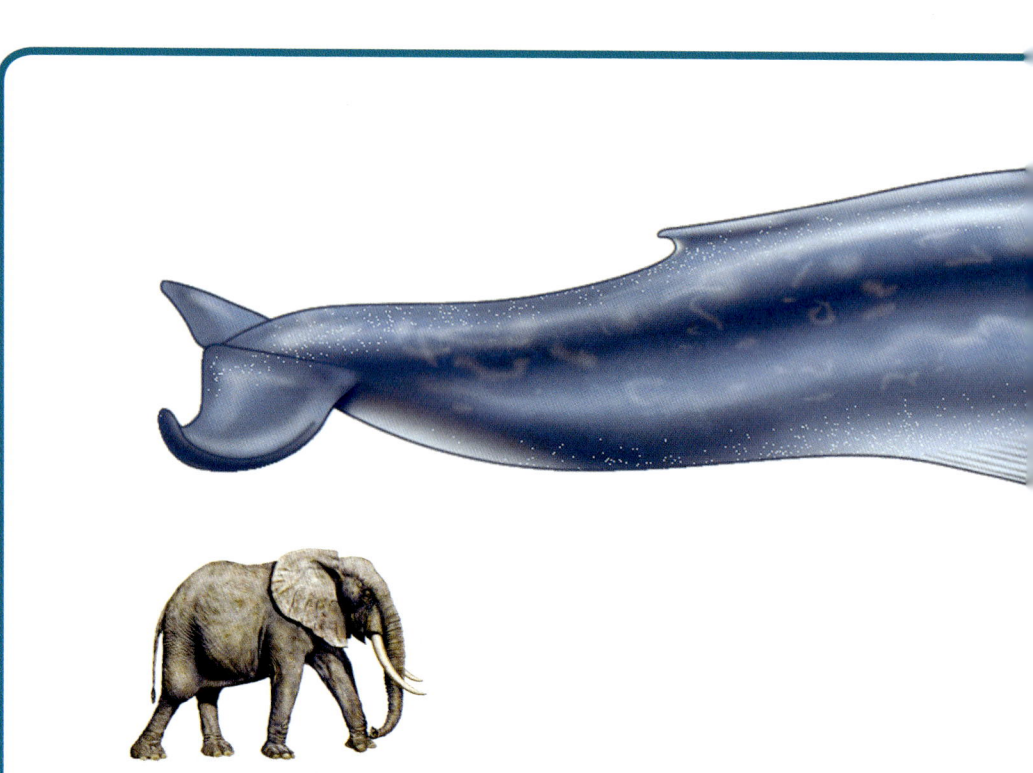

A blue whale is heavy. It weighs around 140 tonnes. That is more than a house!

A blue whale has big body parts. Its heart weighs as much as a small car. Its tongue is huge. It is as heavy as an elephant!

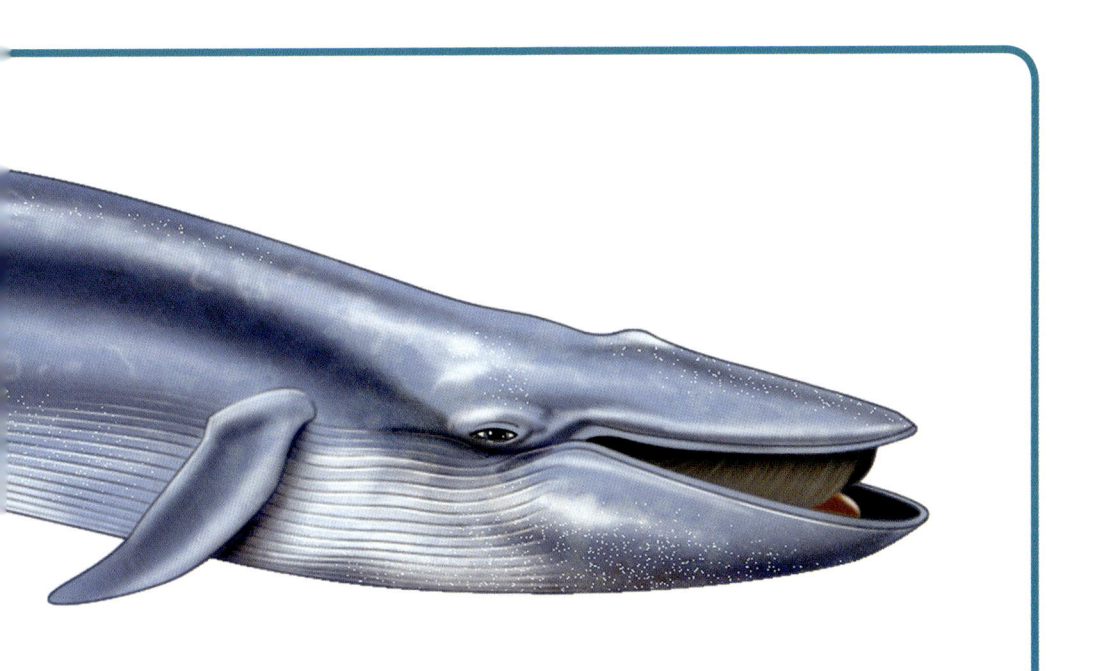

A blue whale has a wide head and small eyes. It has smooth blue-grey skin. Its skin has light spots. Each whale has its own pattern of spots.

fluke

Their bellies can be yellowish. This colour comes from **algae**. They live on a whale's body.

A blue whale's tail has a fluke. It is wide and shaped like a triangle. Whales move their flukes up and down to help them swim.

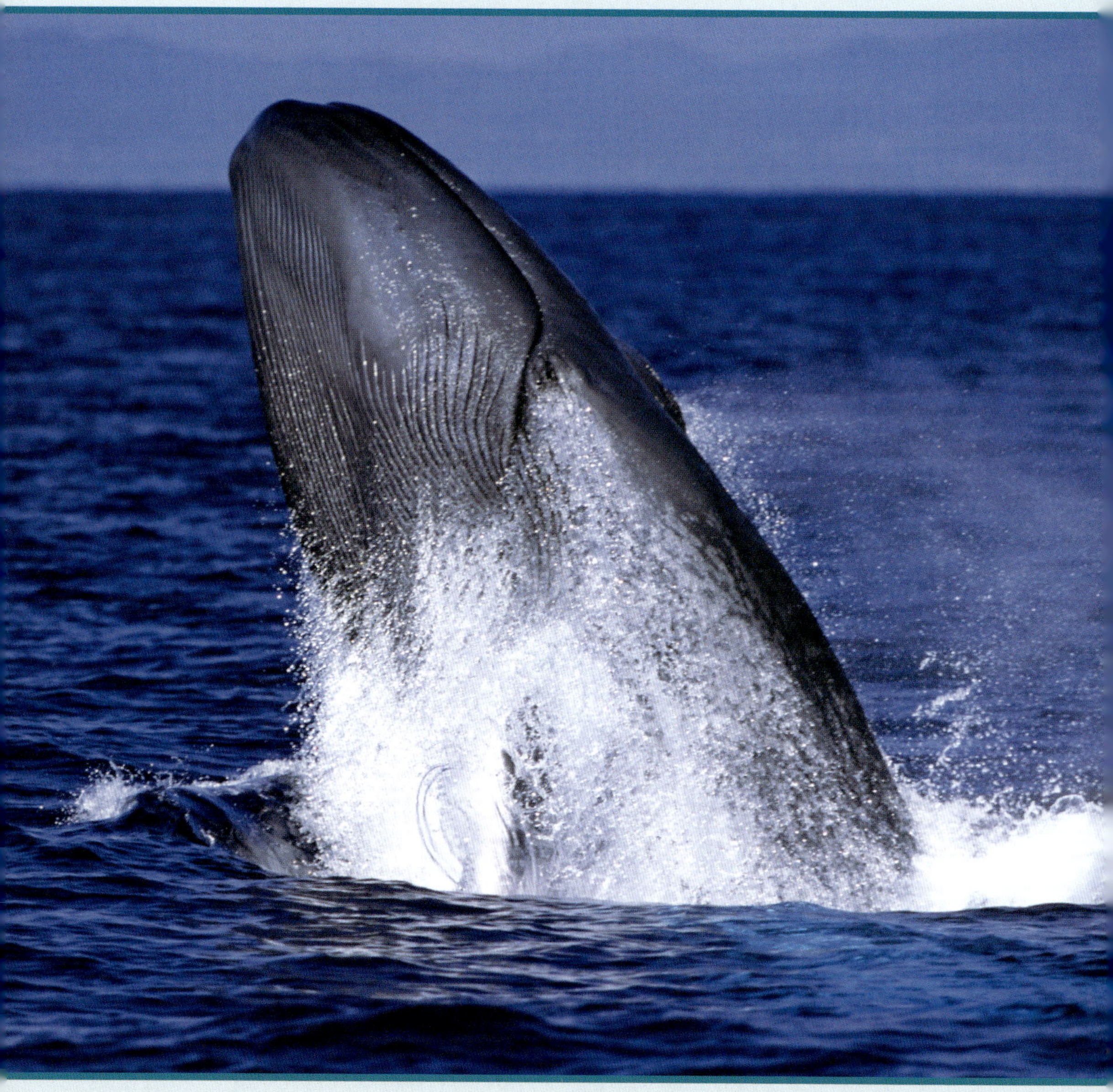

Blue whales have a thick layer of fat called blubber. It is under their skin.

Blubber helps whales in many ways. Ocean water can get cold. Blubber helps whales stay warm. It also stores energy. Sometimes a whale does not eat food for many months. Whales use the energy from the blubber when there is no food. Blubber also helps whales swim. It helps them to float.

Eating and drinking

Blue whales eat small food. They eat tiny animals called **krill**. A blue whale can eat 40 million krill in a day!

Krill float in the ocean.

mouth grooves

How does a blue whale eat so much? Grooves run along its throat and chest. The grooves are long. They let a whale's mouth stretch. It can take in a lot of water and food at one time.

Blue whales are a type of **baleen** whale. They have baleen plates in their mouths. These plates bend. They help whales catch food.

A whale takes a gulp of water and krill. Its tongue pushes out the water. The krill get trapped in the baleen. Then the whale swallows the krill. Gulp!

baleen

Blue whales can twist and roll over. They roll their bodies and keep their mouths open. This helps them to catch krill.

What blue whales do

Blue whales are fast. Their long bodies help them swim.

Blue whales often travel at more than 8 kilometres (5 miles) an hour, but they can swim faster than 32 kilometres (20 miles) an hour if they need to get away from danger.

Blue whales dive to look for food. They dive down more than 91 metres (300 feet). They can hold their breath for more than 10 minutes!

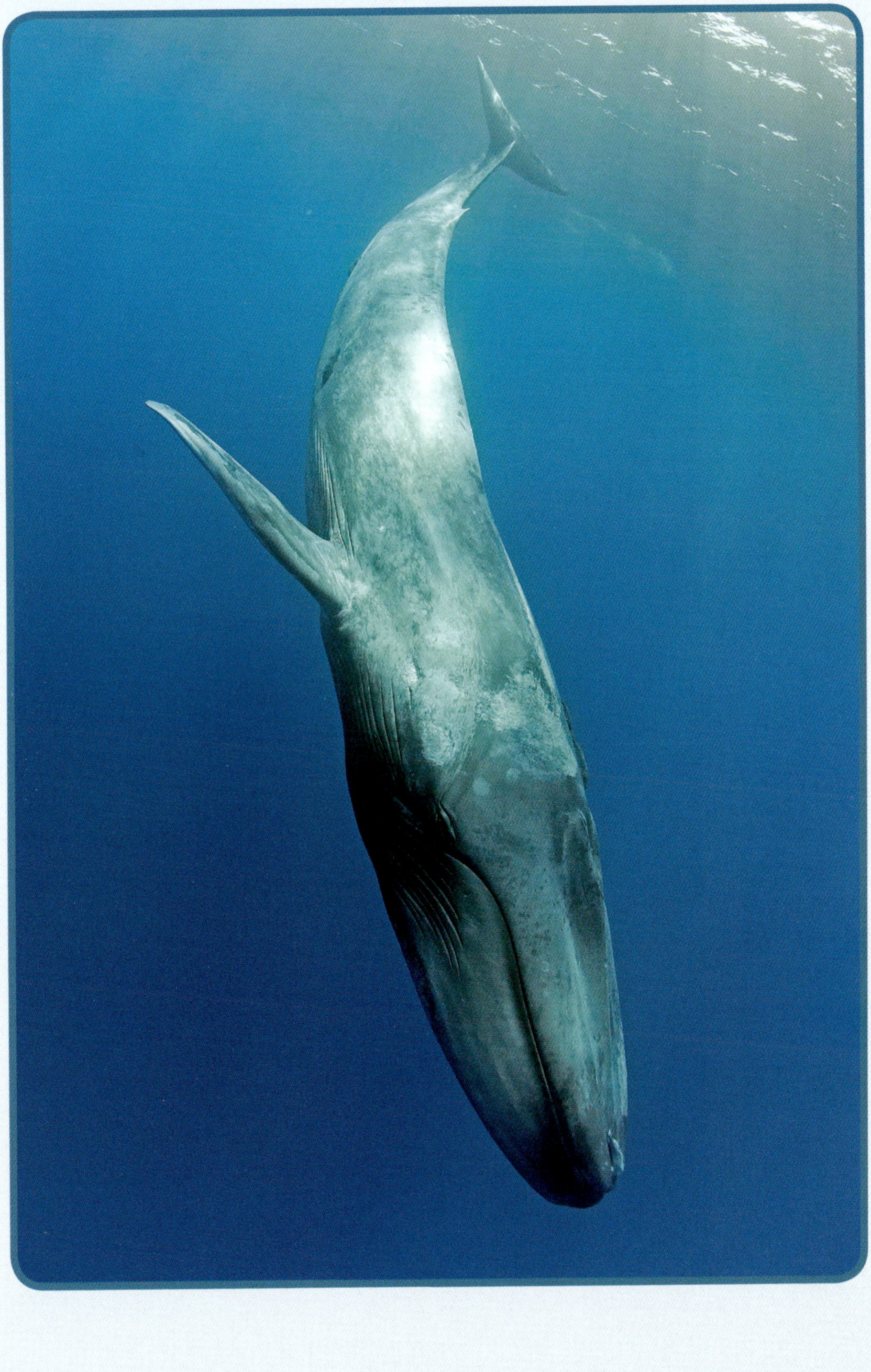

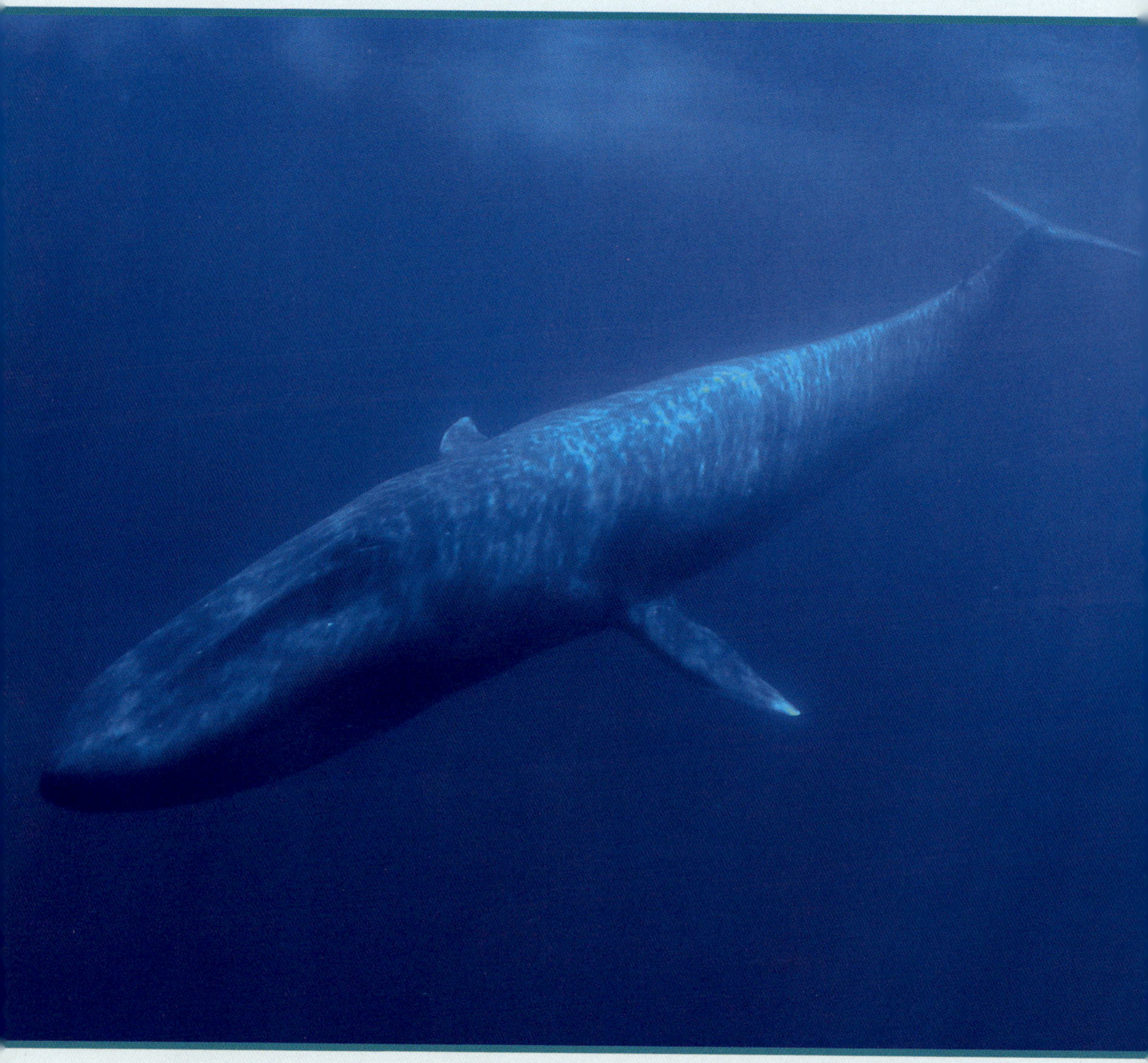

A blue whale is one of the loudest animals in the world. It is louder than a jet engine! Whales make sounds to talk to one another. They moan and groan. They call out. The sounds travel for hundreds of kilometres. Sounds help whales to find mates. Sounds also help whales to find their way as they swim.

Blue whales hear very well. They hear sounds from other whales.

Blue whales are big when they are born. A baby whale is called a calf. A calf can weigh nearly 3 tonnes! It drinks its mother's milk for many months.

It grows quickly. It gains about 91 kilograms (200 pounds) every day during its first year. A whale can mate when it is 5 years old.

Blue whales can live a long time. Some may live for about 80 years.

A mother whale swims with her calf.

Dangers to blue whales

Blue whales were hunted for many years. The number of blue whales fell and they almost died out.

Today, laws protect blue whales. Their numbers are slowly growing.

Blue whales are still **endangered**. They could still die out. Killer whales and sharks attack them. **Pollution** hurts them. Large ships hit them. They can get stuck in fishing gear.

Many people try to keep blue whales safe. They teach others to care about ocean life. They keep rubbish out of the ocean. Groups make safe areas for whales to care for their young. They work hard to make the ocean a better place. People want these great whales to have a safer home.

Fast facts

Name: blue whale

Habitat: ocean

Where in the world (range): all oceans, especially the Southern Ocean

Food: krill

Predators: humans, sharks, killer whales (also called orcas)

Life span: about 80–90 years

Glossary

algae small plants without roots or stems that grow in water

baleen long, fringed plates in the mouths of some whales

blowhole hole on the top of a whale's head; whales breathe air through blowholes

endangered at risk of dying out

krill small, shrimp-like animal

mammal warm–blooded animal that breathes air; mammals have hair or fur; female mammals feed milk to their young

mate join together to produce young

migrate travel to another location

pollution materials that hurt Earth's water, air and land

warm-blooded having a body temperature that stays about the same all the time

Find out more

Books

Ocean A Children's Encyclopedia, DK (DK Children, 2015)

Save the Humpback Whale (Animal SOS), Louise Spilsbury (Raintree, 2019)

Shark vs Killer Whale (Animal Rivals), Isabel Thomas (Raintree, 2017)

Websites

www.bbc.co.uk/cbbc/watch/p00x5hjm
Watch this blue whale encounter!

www.dkfindout.com/uk/animals-and-nature/whales-dolphins-and-porpoises/blue-whale
Learn more about the blue whale and listen to the noise it makes.

https://gowild.wwf.org.uk
Find out more about the world's endangered animals.

Index

baleen plates 18
blowholes 4
blubber 15

dangers 20, 26–28
diving 4, 9, 20

eating 8–9, 15, 16–17, 18, 19, 20
eyes 12

hearing 23

krill 16, 18, 19

life span 24

mammals 4
mating 9, 23, 24
migrating 9
mouths 17, 18, 19

range 6–7

size 10–11, 20, 24
skin 12, 15
sounds 23

tails 13

young 4, 9, 24, 28